Wheels and Cogs

written by Mandy Suhr
and illustrated by Mike Gordon

WAYLAND

First published in Great Britain in 1996
by Wayland (Publishers) Ltd
This edition printed in 2001 by Hodder Wayland

This revised edition published in 2009 by Wayland,
338 Euston Road, London NW1 3BH

Wayland Australia,
Level 17/207 Kent Street, Sydney, NSW 2000

British Library Cataloguing in Publication Data
Suhr, Mandy.
    Wheels and cogs. -- (Simple technology)
    1. Wheels--Juvenile literature. 2. Gearing--Juvenile literature.
    I. Title II. Series
    621.8'11-dc22

ISBN 978-0-7502-5953-8

Printed in China

Wayland is a division of Hachette Children's Books,
an Hachette UK Company www.hachette.co.uk

Contents

Wheels help things to move.
They come in all sizes
and colours.

But they are all
the same shape.

Before wheels were invented, people had
to drag heavy loads across the ground by
pushing or pulling. This was hard work!

Then someone had the bright idea of using tree trunks as rollers. This made moving things around easier.

Try this simple experiment

You will need:

- 2 shoe boxes

- 4 pencils
- 2 weights (the same)
- a piece of chalk

Stage 1

1. Put a weight in each shoebox.

2. Chalk a start line on a table top.

3. Put one box at the line. Push the box.

4. Mark the point where the box stops with your chalk.

Stage 2

1. Lay the second box on the pencil rollers at the start line. Push this box.

2. Mark the point where the box stops.

Which box travelled the farthest and moved more easily?

9

Rollers were the first kind of wheels that people used. Later they cut slices off the rollers to make sets of wheels, which would turn more easily on rough ground.

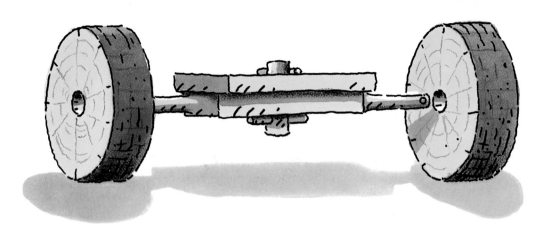

These were joined to an axle and
were used to make the first carts.
Moving things around was now
even easier.

Make your own wheeled cart

You will need:

- scissors
- a glass
- a shoebox
- 2 pencils

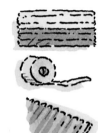

- plasticine
- sticky tape
- corrugated cardboard

1. Use the glass to draw four cardboard wheels. With the help of a grown-up, cut the wheels out.

2. Place the plasticine on the table and the card on top. Punch a hole in the centre of the cardboard wheel using a sharp pencil. Repeat for all wheels.

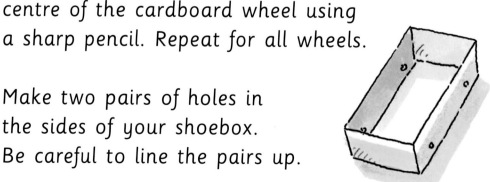

3. Make two pairs of holes in the sides of your shoebox. Be careful to line the pairs up.

4. Slip a wheel on one end of a pencil.

5. Push the other end of the pencil through one pair of holes in the box. Put a wheel on it.

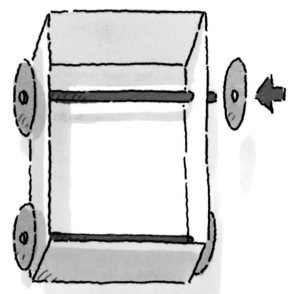

6. Repeat with the other pencil.

7. Tape the ends of the pencils to stop the wheels falling off.

Now test your cart!

One problem with the first wheels was they were heavy because they were made of solid wood. It was difficult for vehicles to move quickly.

The Romans made the
wheel lighter by cutting
out the solid wood in the
centre, and adding spokes.
Vehicles could now go faster.

You still find some modern wheels that are similar to the wheels Romans designed. The centre of the wheel is called the hub.

Spokes join the hub to the rim (the outside of the wheel). The axle fits into the hub, and the wheel turns on the axle.

Many wheels have tyres around the outer rim. Tyres are made from rubber and steel. Tyres have a pattern in the rubber called a tread which grips the surface the wheel is travelling along.

Some tyres have
a special tread.

The tyres of a tractor stop the
wheels sinking into soft earth.

Different wheels are designed to do different jobs. Lorries have big wide wheels because they have to carry heavy loads.

Bicycle wheels have fine spokes that are very light, so the bicycle can go fast.

Look at the
wheels around
you. How do
they suit the
job they do?

Some wheels are called cogs or gearwheels.
They have 'teeth' around the outside.
The teeth of the cogs
can mesh so that
when you turn just
one wheel, other
wheels turn, too!

Make a set of cogs

You will need:

- a shoebox lid
- two split pins
- cardboard (to make the cogs)

1. Use template 1 on page 29 to cut out two identical cardboard cogs.
2. Fasten one to the shoebox lid with a split pin. The cog must be loose enough to turn.
3. Place the other cog next to the first, so that the teeth mesh. Fasten it to the lid.
4. Turn one of the cogs. Can you see the other cog turn, too?

All sorts of everyday machines use cogs.

When you pedal a bicycle, you turn a large cog. This is attached by a chain to a smaller cog that turns the wheels. The cogs move energy from the pedals to the wheels.

With the help of a grown-up, put a bicycle upside down and slowly turn the pedal. Which moves faster, the big cog or the little cog, the pedal or the wheel?

Use templates 1 and 2 on page 29 to join a large cog to a small cog. (Follow the steps on page 23.)

When the cogs are in position draw a line on each cog at '12 o'clock'.

Look at the lines to find out how many times the smaller cog turns for every time the big cog turns.

Glossary

Axle   The shaft or rod on which a wheel turns.

Cog   A toothed gearwheel.

Energy   The power to do work.

Hub   The centre of a wheel.

Load   The weight of the object that is moved by a machine.

Pedal   A lever you press with your foot.

Rim   The outer edge of a wheel.

Spoke   A bar or rod which runs from the centre to the rim of a wheel.

Tread   The pattern of grooves on a tyre which helps it to grip the road.

Tyre   A rubber hoop which fits around the rim of a wheel.

Templates for pages 23/27

1. Trace or photocopy these shapes
2. Glue them to some card
3. Cut them out
4. Bend the tabs

5. Pin the shapes to a piece of card

Notes for adults

Simple Technology is a series of elementary books designed to introduce children to the everyday machines which make all of our lives easier, and the basic principles behind them.

For millions of years people have been inventing and using machines to make work easier. These machines have been constantly modified and redesigned over the years to make them more sophisticated and more successful at their task. This is really what technology is all about. It is the process of applying knowledge to make work easier.

In these books, children are encouraged to explore the early inspirations for machines and the process of modification which has brought them forward to their current state, and in so doing, come to an understanding of the design process.

The simple text and humorous illustrations give a clear explanation of how these machines actually work and experiments and activities give suggestions for further practical exploration.

Suggestions for further activities

*   Make a collection of wheels, including magazine cutouts and drawings of those around you. Discuss size and shape and how this relates to function.

*   Encourage children to use lego and other construction kits to design and make wheeled vehicles. This kind of experimentation is an essential part of the design process.

* Encourage children to identify a design need and respond to this by designing on paper, constructing and testing out a model vehicle, which can then be modified and improved upon.

* Explore the principle of friction and how this affects movement along a surface. Test out vehicles an different surfaces. Record and analyse results.

* Design and make a model which uses cogs to move energy from one part of a machine to another.

Further information

Amazing Science: Forces and Motion by Sally Hewitt (Wayland, 2007)

Little Bees: Push it, Pull it by Claire Llewellyn (Wayland, 2009)

Simple Machines: Wheels by Chris Oxlade (Franklin Watts, 2007)

Ways into Technology: On Wheels by Richard and Louise Spilsbury (Franklin Watts, 2008)

Adult Reference

The Way Things Work by David Macaulay and Neil Ardley (Dorling Kindersley, 2004)

Index